Arthur Bull
After

After
© 2025 Arthur Bull

Cover design: Rebekah Wetmore, using an untitled painting by Ruth Bull.
Editor: Andrew Wetmore
ISBN: 978-1-998149-95-7
First edition August, 2025

Moose House Publications
2475 Perotte Road Annapolis County, NS B0S 1A0
moosehousepress.com / info@moosehousepress.com

Moose House Publications recognizes the support of the Province of Nova Scotia. We are pleased to work in partnership with the Department of Communities, Culture and Heritage to develop and promote our cultural resources for all Nova Scotians.

We live and work in Mi'kma'ki, the ancestral and unceded territory of the Mi'kmaw People. This territory is covered by the "Treaties of Peace and Friendship" which Mi'kmaw and Wolastoqiyik (Maliseet) People first signed with the British Crown in 1725. The treaties did not deal with surrender of lands and resources but in fact recognized Mi'kmaq and Wolastoqiyik (Maliseet) title and established the rules for what was to be an ongoing relationship between nations. We are all Treaty people.

Also by Arthur Bull

And available from Moose House

500 Sentences

Skidmark Calligraphy

While Looking out at the Bay

Introduction

Catullus[1] introduces his collection of poems with the line

> *Cui dono lepidum novum libellum*
> *arido modo pumice expolitum?*
> To whom should I present this little book
> of carefully polished poems?

For Catullus, the answer to this question was one person: his patron, Cornelius. In the case of the present collection, the answer is also one person: you, the reader.

This is not to just suggest that my modest poems belong anywhere near the genius of Catullus, except for one similarity between our two collections: both contain a great diversity of poetic forms, as well as very broad range of themes and topics.

It is impossible to know what led Catullus to work with so any different modes. For myself, I can say a few words about how my own book ended up the way is, since it is all about how the poems were written.

---

1   Poet of the late Roman Republic, who lived between 84 and 54 BCE.

It happened in three phases. First, there was six-month period of intense writing that filled dozens of journals with notes, sketches, dream narratives, essays and much else. The second phase consisted of months of winnowing this material (which happened concurrently with five months of travel in Asia), discarding much of it and keeping only the few poems that seemed worth it at the time. Finally, there was a long period of editing and shaping what I kept into something resembling a book of poems.

The result of this protracted writing process is the variegated collection you now hold in your hands. You may notice recurring themes that run below the surface, something like rhizomes that hold seemingly-separate lily pads as a single organism. These may or may not be important to your enjoyment of the poems. I will leave that for you, my reader, to decide.

This collection would not have come about without the kind support and advice of Moose House Publications. In particular, I would like to gratefully acknowledge the encouragement of Brenda Thompson and the keen editorial guidance and insight of Andrew Wetmore. A huge thank-you goes out to both.

AB
July, 2025

After

Arthur Bull

Decisions

Arthur Bull

I

The inner structure of the universe
is a dense fabric of decisions

made in the narrowest of moments
folded into the tiniest folds of time.

In a breakaway, a shooter's eyes
meet a goalie's eyes, like tapping

the wall to find a hollow, one
false move, one head fake opens

a gap in attention wide enough
for a puck. Or that interval before

Arthur Bull

lips meet, one decision and two
lives are changed forever (or almost

forever). A single-cell organism
decides to move toward light.

What is the essential spirit
of movement but the current

of choices? Touch a nerve,
pluck a string, clap your hands

and you've made an invisible
tear in the flowing fabric of time.

A creek never arrives directly
at the ocean: First it has to join

a river. You know you are near
the temple when you hear the bell

sounding through the forest. Even
if it never appears in any poem

it signals that a decision awaits
to sweep a path strewn with petals.

II

The only rule for driving through a blizzard
is don't lose your nerve and keep your mind
tuned to the road, saying yes again
and again resisting even one distraction

Of a single doubt that would lift the purchase
of the wheels on ice and send you skating
in wide arcs and circles into the white
forever. A body of light needs no permission.

The low drone that holds earth to sky
needs no excuse to release and let slip.
Don't stop, just listen for the unheard
voices whispering through the snow

Not the impossible chorus of doubters
swelling their praise of tragic accidents,
Just say yes and then say yes again.
And second biggest decision is the one

when you decide you can't do it
there just is not the wherewithal
and the biggest decision you make
is when you choose just to say yes.

III

"Don't know my future, sure don't know my past"

Willie Brown, *Future Blues*

He doesn't pretend to know the future
and even the past is a mystery to him.
Sure, the narrative will always unfold
just the way the Coasters describe it:

*"And then, and then...eh, eh...and then
along came Jones"* The universe always
improvising delicately arranged
bouquets of tiny decisions shaping

Itself in the most exquisite ways,
pure intention bursting at the seams

as dancers in coloured blouses
circle Orpheus with his cardboard lyre.

A sudden nor'easter can blow you off course
easily sending you straight to the bottom.
We hold our choices close to the vest
hoping our hopes will somehow save us.

Our features get gradually smoothed out.
Everyone will go but me, you say when
the moon breaks open and petals of light
pour through the cracks to illuminate

every delusion. The universe says 'go ahead'
the shuttle slides easily through the warp
a single thread might not be all that important
but without it there will be no blanket.

IV

Forget all your troubles get happy.
You'll be leaving them behind soon
anyway. And no one much will care
one way or the other. Today's green
is greener than yesterday's green
and yesterday's blue is not as blue
as tomorrow's. Spring has completed
its work for the year. The white dandelion
parachutes have just about all flown away.
Go ahead. Get happy. There's nothing
stopping you. There's no other choice.

V

Once broken years ago
and hastily repaired
the teapot is veined with
cracks that spread
their black capillaries,
the map of a lifetime
of bad decisions
that fork at every choice
flowing this way and that
with a sure logic of loss
and gain. to go this way
not the other to recall
this thing but forget that
thing, how it felt just then
to have been there in that

Arthur Bull

moment now to realize
you'll never choose it
again. What's torn, mended,
torn and mended again.
a cracked roadmap of all
that I projected on the world
on other people and even
onto myself ruining everything,
but the cracks neither ruin
the teapot nor improve it
its beauty now rests only
in the attention of the mend.

VI

Beavers are building a megaproject
across the road, flooding the woods
hated by farmers and landowners
for drowning their fields and properties
unstoppable engineers planning
first the dam, then the lodge,
felling trees and branches then
dragging them along paths
that flood to become canals.
This is your real green economy
creating new wetlands for fish,
reptiles, birds, water bugs.
So many decisions to be made,
so much planning and knowledge,
so much training needed for the two
kits, the new ones, to prepare them to go
out on their own to start new projects.

Arthur Bull

Is it also a great historical enterprise
fraught with deep mythical meaning;
revenge for the fur trade's slaughter
from some deeply buried memory
of the time when history barged in
with its steel, whiskey and profits
for a vain fashion in men's top hats
(the perfect marriage of stupidity and cupidity)?
decimating them all the way
from here to the Mackenzie Delta,
destroying a key ecological agent
destroying so much wetland habitat,
destroying a great totem protector
spirit whose subtle body performed
ritual dance with humans for millennia,
destroying a world to create a nation.
Perhaps not, perhaps building
is just what they do, unstoppably
making one decision at a time,
telling their dreams one stick at time

VII

I arrived in advance
of all my decisions
and I will leave after
every decision
has been made
and not one remains.
Still, I worry about what
will happen to my books
after I am dead and gone.

Arthur Bull

Some places

Arthur Bull

We ate smelts and chicken livers
cooked on an electric frying pan
in our bedsitter. We read Trollope
out loud to each other. We made
love every night and in the daytime
on the weekend. You cleaned houses
and I loaded conduit pipe on trucks.
We drank in basement bars.
We found a 78 by Meade Lux Lewis
at the Sally Ann. We filled
our backpacks with library books.
We heard funk bands on Gottingen
and Texas swing at the Legion.
We waited for the bus in knife-sharp
North Atlantic corner winds.
We had no tv radio or telephone.

Arthur Bull

Then we escaped to France for a year
and traded one bedsitter for another
also tiny bedsitter in Montpellier
with only two cassettes, one by Miles
Davis and one by Duke Ellington.
You painted watercolours
and I played guitar every morning
then walked under the aqueduct
where Manitas de Plata, the greatest
living flamenco guitarist, played pétanque,
to buy our lunch at the market.
we were living our best days
without even ever knowing it.

In 1970: these were our songs, in sequence:
Ain't No Way
Me and Bobby McGee
A Bridge Over Troubled Waters
If You Could Read My Mind
The Thrill is Gone
Raindrops Keep Falling on My Head

We drove across Canada
in a Chevy Impala convertible,
dropped acid in the Rockies
and ate pancakes in Revelstoke.

We slept together
in each others' arms
under some bushes

Arthur Bull

in Stanley Park
Let It Be

We necked in the back of Bassel's
on Yonge Street under the curved walls
with their art deco friezes of jiving
couples until a waiter. a proper
waiter in a waistcoat and tie, comes
and politely hints that our behaviour
might be a little untoward.

Arthur Bull

We ate most of our meals at Switzer's—
always corned beef on rye and a coke,
below the apartment where they say
Emma Goldman once briefly lived
and probably ordered the same lunch.

I thought you would be here forever
that was my plan anyway I thought
 your dry laugh would always be
in the room, cutting through all
pretension or fakery. I thought
we would have time to find ourselves
and each other again. Now my days
are like shadows of rocks along the shore
waiting for the flood tide to return
waiting to be covered by the cold
foamy white of the incoming surf.

Arthur Bull

Sailing Alone around the World
might be the loneliest title of all

except Slocum seldom betrays
his solitude, offering it instead

only to the wide-open sea.
What we went through together

was almost unbelievable.
And how we made it through.

How we almost didn't make it.
All my opinions have kept on

trying to convince me (but failing)
that the world was not alive

all around us all the time
this was happening. We had magic

in our eyes all the time while
all this was happening. so unsure

of ourselves and yet we seemed
possessed by some kind of sacred force.

I tell myself: this time I won't swerve away
from the hurt of saying goodbye.

And we both knew well how to steer
from that hurt into the forgetting.

I run my fingers over the yarn
of your brightly woven blanket

Arthur Bull

tracing flamboyant figures in the air
you, humming a tune to yourself somewhere.

Like the patterns running through basalt
along your beloved shore, our bodies

were imprinted on each other's.
Years and decades just went by.

Drinking beer in the backyard
listening to Ornette, as happy

then as we would ever be, and now
as I look out on waves that swell

on the distant bay out to the horizon, you
are both so present and so terribly far away.

Arthur Bull

We visited Du Fu's thatched cottage in Chengdu
where you posed for a snapshot garlanded
in a grotto by scholars' rocks, looking up
filled with the wonder that was the signature
that you signed onto world before you left.

We went to Stratford
even though your hip
was so bad you could
barely get on and off
the train. We saw Lepage's
Coriolanus
a magic enactment
of this murderous age,
and talked about it
far into the night,
about the world ending
in what was in fact
our own world ending.

Arthur Bull

I will say goodbye now
without sadness,
at least that's my plan.

the truth however
might be a little different:
I turn my face toward

the hills to hide my tears.
Toward some new life
in some foreign city.

A rocky overhanging ledge
leans toward its reflection
on the clear lake with cheerful

sunlight dancing in wavelets
ready to go anywhere ready
for to fade as the singer says

unburdened by love, alone
those hot coals now cooled
tight emotions unclenched

the slow opening of petals
like getting acquainted again
with the local spirits and gods

who have always been here
in my back dooryard living
among the perennials that

you planted so long ago,
a painter's returning garden
where every flower never forgets.

Arthur Bull

Secrets

Arthur Bull

I

When the keeping of secrets once told is broken
their pieces enter the Gulf Stream of language

Rafts of parables on the floating world
break free from their rotting pylons

a great white heron goes riding
the Chao Phraya aboard an island

of plastic bottles, lotus flowers and rope
floating debris follows the flight paths

brightly woven across the night sky.
Even those betrayed confidences

Arthur Bull

that weighed on us while we walked in
the walled garden, neither of us speaking

This ornamental writing, coiled and spiralling,
whose attention holds the world in place

is finally released into the atmosphere.
Let it go, you want to say, and good riddance.

II

Once spoken out loud there's no going back
a song can begin as innocently as McCartney's

"Listen, do you want to know a secret? Do you
promise not to tell?" Hearing those three words

her heart never recovers from, not because of 'love'
but because of 'promise', how its weight

sits on your chest as you slowly wake up.
If you tell a secret, it's no longer a secret.

III

if you promise not to tell you know perfectly
well that the promise has already been broken

for you to have heard it at all. Better to just hold
it so as to make it your own and no one else's.

'Won't repression push down and damage
something in our life?" Not really, because

it's only yours, even as it wears you down,
gradually, like waves against a sandstone cliff

allowing for the occasional gale, but not that bad,
the slow erosion of holding onto your secret.

Handrail

Arthur Bull

After all these
years I'm surprised

to find myself
still uncertain

tightly holding
a worn handrail

of habit and hope
as though that was

some guarantee
of safe passage

Arthur Bull

some gold standard
that props up an old

and failing currency.
But I do admit

what's better now
is that I don't care

very much anymore
about being certain

Unreliable narratives

Arthur Bull

I

The day's tawny coyote came in sniffing around my door and left its
meaning as a scent too fine for detection by humans.

The whale carcass that lay stinking on the beach awaiting scientists
to extract meaning and funerary data from between the vaulted ceiling of
its ribs.

Because the meaning was both more direct and more opaque,
          no one would ever have noticed
it, or cared and even if they did nothing ever happened

Great efforts were made, at every level of interpretation,
          to find its meaning,
but no, really nothing was there, not even the faintest whiff of

55

Arthur Bull

   the memory
of curiosity.

A message without a bottle is not like a telegraph without wires,
   which must have
been mind-blowing; in the 50s we were sure Smell-o-Vision was
   on its way.

While I was deep in the woods an emergency warning starts
   to make a loud buzzing sound
on my cell phone, followed by a recorded announcement:
   citizens are advised to remain in place, which explains its meaning.

II

I'm sorting my impressive collection
of dictionaries of words with no definition
and guidebooks to places that don't exist.

You can't withdraw from the world
if you've never been part of it.
You just live with it, being in one

and belonging to another. Rain,
dark street, silvered pavement,
someone standing in the shadows

wearing a raincoat. This is it,
no matter how wrong it feels.
and not at all what you planned for

Arthur Bull

in your mind-wandering fantasies
or more than you ever bargained for
but better than you ever dreamed of.

III

At Inuvik airport the security guard said
'Is that an artifact or a belonging?'

As if to say 'Are those real poems
or just crumpled-up grocery lists?'

Or even to say 'Were you that person,
or just the unsmiling face in a class photo?'

Or even: 'Do you own this life, or are you
just a tenant getting behind in your rent?'

After a slight pause I gave my answer:
'It is an artifact, but it is *my* artifact.'

IV

There was a project in the 1950s
to capture the essence of moonlight,
so as to harness its familiar and
powerful energies. Experiments
were done in secret, like reading
a thousand lines of poetry a day.
Gradually, the poetry component
got replaced by alabaster models
with gesturing hands that reflected
the moonlight. Later on, seeking
more permanence, they found
a way to capture moonlight
in small containers called 'kisses'.
After two years the project was cancelled
because the lead scientist eloped

with the mother of the principal investigator.
The project had other spontaneous
effects, but there was never any real
advance in our understanding
of what a little moonlight can do.

V

The Specific Ocean was discovered in 1843 but has since been lost track of.

Dolphins, in spite of their immense intelligence, have never produced a decent bass player.

The sequence of emotions in the first two seconds of an earthquake holds the world record for mental speed.

Wood ticks have a strong ethic of self-reliance and individualism, but are weak in the area of social and political solidarity.

The undertaker wore expensive wing tip shoes because his feet were always on show when he stepped on the foot pedal that lowers that coffin to the crematorium.

There is a little-known voluntary organization that is dedicated to gleaning the language of all unnecessary adverbs.

A new Canadian national myth was being proposed, in which God apologizes for the shoddy workmanship in its construction, but thanks us for our work anyway.

Shoals of minnows can cloud the brain.

The labour that oxen contributed to building this country is immeasurable and unrecognized.

Every word has a saturation point when its meaning begins to overflow.

The unlikelihood of being a person at all was compared to the rarest and most valued minerals known to geology.

Arthur Bull

Equation

Arthur Bull

In the consciousness of the infinite
the conscious subject has for its
object the infinite of its own nature.

I was trying to map a sphere
onto a straight line by placing
equidistant points along it

for infinity in both directions
and then combining all
the points into one point,

Later on I found myself
in a long corridor with high
windows that overlooked
a sun-lit, snow-filled valley.
No matter how many times

Arthur Bull

you weigh a diamond

Its weight will never become
a measure of its worth.
Many leave, few come back.

It's not like there's a choice.
The steeple of the village church
was their compass pointing to

a straight course toward the Good.
but once you left, you were lost,
destined to wander the earth

singing the old songs about home.
Yet how wonderful it all was, even
though it was, and is, also a living hell

Roma

Arthur Bull

I

Stolen moments
broken memories

a mountain of shards
of smashed amphorae

Monte Testaccio
each bit of pottery

now without shape
or volume or olive oil

the caves around its base
now have all-night discos.

Arthur Bull

and one antiquarian
bookstore that owns one

Eighteenth Century edition
of Horace's *Odes*

in which each poem holds
one folded pocket of light

and one lock of blonde hair
someone pressed inside

as an offering to Venus
of great loves passed

a lost citation of love
all the tiny islands

In the Tiber centuries
of love found and lost

The fading bells
 from Santa Cecilia

through the evening air
the broken memories

swirling high above
like a cloud of starlings

II

One of their gods was a heavy-lidded criminal
with a cigarette in the corner of his mouth.

Not what I'd expected. No one spoke
for quite a while. We sipped our drinks

From time to time. Finally he said
'I have what you asked for, but I can't

Say what it is.' The last blue was fading
into evening. A woman's silhouette

Appeared against it. By the time darkness
was complete we were alone again.

just me and that ancient goddess
formerly known as the Blonde Venus.

III

On a Trastevere bridge two girls were leaning,
raindrops forming on their plastic raincoats

Like flowers the rain-silvered street
Glistens like a memory of exile

no thought of the hardships that await
only kisses of still excited hopes

without beginning or end some things
you are able notice only through tears

with words still ringing in your ears.
old stories fade in the river mist

when your feet touch the earth again
you know you've crossed to Trastevere

Arthur Bull

Music

Arthur Bull

At the temple gate
the music is almost

deafening: with heavily
amplified reeds & gongs:

sometimes the job
of music is simply

to keep evil spirits
from entering the temple.

Arthur Bull

Promise

Arthur Bull

The sun is trying to come out, people say,
giving our local star an A for effort.

Meanwhile, the real sun is preoccupied
with making a woodcut of village rooftops

in a neat and modest arrangement
gradually draining daylight from the day

take down the blanket over the window
it says, I'll try to be out by tomorrow noon.

Arthur Bull

Vase

Arthur Bull

Through wooden slats

      the sunlight holds

gold bars of brightness

      that cut through

the slow swirling dust

      music is coming

from a radio somewhere

from another world

cigarette smoke

twisting silk

the background

chatter of conversation

clinking of glasses

deep and blank

we were empty

vessels waiting

to be filled

        someday you will watch

someone putting flowers

        into a vase

as you lie in your hospital bed

        unable to speak and

be filled with wonder

        at having been human

Arthur Bull

I was sitting

Arthur Bull

I was sitting in a taverna in Cervantes's Spain
where I could hardly hear myself think above
the din of arguments and rattle of castanets
clapping and heels clicking. then suddenly
the silence of cherry blossoms in springtime
Kyoto filled the frame with unfathomable
happiness; if I was waiting for a reply that
was never going to come, if I was awakened
by the crows whose night was already over,
then I was allowed to run away and no one
cared in the end whether I stayed or disappeared
into my woodlot one day, or went wandering
over rocky deserts, a fugitive, from city to city
living outside the human world, and endless
waiting and talking beyond the walls of Colonus

Arthur Bull

After Reading *Republic*

Arthur Bull

The promise of torchlit bareback horse races
was the one attraction worth staying on for.
Other attractions lay hidden between the two
dark blue covers of the Oxford Edition,
buried under paragraphs, pages and lines
of words, their little shapes curling upwards
 like smoke embroidering the papyrus,
always asking 'What is justice?' or maybe
'What is energy?' or 'What is love?" Words
go flowing like moving wrinkles on a creek
below a bridge, always standing still with
cars occasionally rushing over. We have time
to tease out all those contradictions
and some of delusions as well, waiting
to go out to see the races, uncovering
question by question, the blinding truth
of justice at the heart of the human heart.

Arthur Bull

Notes on Democracy

Arthur Bull

The ostraca
was somebody
whose name
got scratched
on a potsherd
a character
indicating his
nomination
for exile forever.
If belonging
to the polis is
so important
what is this longing,
always to leave
that never leaves?

Arthur Bull

Does your great desire
for freedom also
include freedom from
the contagious virus of
your unrelenting anger?

Voting does not
guarantee that
the majority
cannot be wrong
only that voting
alone without
the weight of
true public
participatory
deliberation
very seldom
can get it right.

Arthur Bull

A circle is never broken from the inside
because then insiders wouldn't be insiders.

or from the outside because outside
no one can find any way to get in

or even to imagine what's inside. Both
insiders and outsiders will later

come to realize there never was an inside
nor an outside nor was there ever a circle

For democratic decisions
draw a circle and close it
to make decisions democratic
break it open again.

Arthur Bull

Equality without difference
Is bad equality.
Difference without equality
Is bad difference.

There is no such thing as
a multipolar world
any more than the earth
can have several poles
in addition to North
Pole and South Pole.
when you add more it
automatically
becomes a network.

Arthur Bull

Stop saying low man
on the totem pole.
Totem poles are not
power hierarchies.
they are stories about
beings from this and
other worlds that tell
about their ways and
how they came about
There's no need for you
to express your need
for domination here.
Also the poles don't have
men on them anyway.

Although it is also
a stack of whole
and broken lines
a hexagram
is never a
hierarchy
with upper lines
dominant
over lower lines.
However there is
always a line
that governs all
the other lines
which can be
any line except
the top line or
the bottom line.

Arthur Bull

No one gets to decide
where or when they are born
but this decides almost
everything that follows.
A true democracy
modestly attempts
to say that this won't be
the only deciding factor.

Bracelet

Arthur Bull

The moon laid a jade bracelet
on the mantelpiece and turning
began to speak in a slow
deliberate fashion as though
there was something crucially
important for me to grasp right then.
The whole time she was speaking
I stood there knowing exactly
what it was but couldn't say it
out loud because I knew that
I'd never find the words for it.

Arthur Bull

Stranger

Arthur Bull

We caught a glimpse of him through a crack in the weathered door

his face was like a sandstone cliff continuously eaten by waves

his body was like snow, ploughed and piled in a white mountain

His stare was attenuated to wavelengths that do not exist

to any of the senses except through the nose of a dog

we watched him for a long time unable to look away as though

we knew we were in a dream but were afraid to wake up.

Arthur Bull

Freight

Arthur Bull

What weighs down

your body

in itself

has no weight.

Be happy:

it is the same

weight that holds

down everything

else in the world

and keeps it all

from floating away.

it is the same

as the weight

of a child

on your shoulders.

the same weight

as your life

that is to say

it is weightless.

I have smothered the love in my heart enough times
to know the buried ache and familiar pang

that keeps holding on tight but will not speak.

Never again, never again, it wants to say.
never ever to see you again, but never is still

too much to bear, and once again I fail and fall.

Arthur Bull

Poem

Arthur Bull

She walks in,
the room lights up.

One gesture goes
right through me

like a scythe
through grass.

Unbroken twittering
of nesting birds

cranks up to ten
and fills the sky.

Arthur Bull

Clouds break apart,
blinding sunlight

asks me when
did this happen

and why does it
hold you so tightly?

Remnant

Arthur Bull

A random Greek vocab card
falls out of Carruth's *Scrambled Eggs
 and Whiskey,* one lost remnant
from another life long ago
through a thick morass of hopes
and dreams I'd forgotten. I filled
my life with failure and filled
my time with self-delusion.
The word that fell was Χρόνος
which in English means time.

Arthur Bull

Ferment

Arthur Bull

Loneliness can turn
one way or the other

loneliness can lean
inward or outward

loneliness can taste
bitter or bittersweet

it can be a bacteria
that makes you wretch

or a bacteria that
cultivates yogourt

Arthur Bull

it can turn a batch
of beer into vinegar

you always choose
one or the other

but in the end
it might not matter

after all it was vinegar
soaked in a sponge

that was pressed
onto the cracked

and dried-out lips
of a dying god

Colour Plates

Arthur Bull

There was an age, some other age almost out of reach of memory
when some stories were so grand they had to be presented to children
bound in heavy hardcover editions. The plots of those adventures,
mostly read aloud, swept through our imaginations at bedtime
and right into our dreams. *The Deerslayer, Kidnapped, Treasure Island,*
Hurlburt's Stories from the Bible, Swiss Family Robinson. Their plots
mostly lost to us now except as scattered episodes, characters
absorbed in the swirl of lives gone by.

      Instead, what remains are the colour
plates by NC Wyeth. JR Wyss and some other great illustrators.
Three pirates, one brandishing a cutlass, one with two pistols
and one hoisting the jolly roger, or Jesus entering Jerusalem
on a donkey, or a gigantic boa constrictor coiled around
another donkey. But more than the images it is the colours
in those plates that still hold us, the way certain memories
stand out against the black-and-white narratives that we tell ourselves

like stones in a stream preserving stillness, the painterly hand and brush recalling us to the grand adventure of all that we once were.

Joggins Fossil Cliffs

Arthur Bull

Like water bugs skimming the surface
that leave the shallowest of ripples

The parking lot is full. Small knots
of tourists follow their tour guide

along the beach below the steep
cliffs, her voice almost absorbed

in the white noise of the surf except
for the odd word: carboniferous,

coal age, Lyell, Permian. Above them
the red rock weeps spring water.

What was once alive is present to us
from the very beginnings of life itself

Arthur Bull

only as imprint on lifeless stone.
The gentle pulse of the waves tells us

we are alive in the same continuous
common wave of living experience

a boundless ocean of dark currents
with numbers too immense to grasp

our edge silently passing through time
always looking for a new beginning

What was alive one hundred million
years ago and what's alive now leaving

finely detailed characters as fossils
the last remaining memories of love.

The afternoon light begins drawing down
its long shadow over the Joggins Cliffs.

Lake Midway Notes

Arthur Bull

Dandelion parachutes
spread funereal white
starlike spores ready
to travel through deep
space and back to earth
to bring a coded birth
from beyond so perfect
in design their frailty forms
a syntax that is only heard
the first time quivering
on the edge of death so
as to contain all future
life, floating mandalas
near extinction carrying
their scratchy speech
in a rough-tongued dialect

Arthur Bull

whose floating consonants
remember lost languages.

Sparrowhawk, your scope
of vision cuts out
circles in the field

larger not because
more distant or more
detailed (fieldmouse)

or even because
it's impossibly
hard for our visual

fields to ever find
each other but
because your circuit

Arthur Bull

manifests the limits
of your capacity.
We can never dream

of meeting in some
other world: we have
to meet in this one,

when the limits of
our capacities
form concentric circles

hanging far above
or standing far below
both equidistant.

Wood crackling in the stove
consumes old memories

past winter nights, us reading
Pope's *Iliad* out loud. This same

warmth eased our hearts' ache
in a steady pulse of couplets

Now it warms the same kitchen
again, but for one person only.

Deep inside a snowstorm
ghost shapes on windowpanes,

Arthur Bull

wind whistling through cracks,
snow piling deeper in the night,

I trudge out to get more wood
from the woodshed you built

out of scraps of lumber and
discarded campaign signs

and carry back an armful
of firewood for the stove.

What was real and what is real
become entangled in the wind

whipping the frozen tall grass
like a battle scene from Homer.

wave upon wave rising with
Takamitsu's surging score

and now heroic noise and violent clashes
are silent as the stove's white ashes.

Arthur Bull

I can fill my tin cup
from the rushing stream

or from the little half-
dried-up creek.

It really does not make
any difference to me:

The amount of water
 is exactly the same.

Wild roses are invading my hillside pasture
clogging the path to the blackberry patch

where we went early Septembers to pick
our winter's berries, the four of us filling

yogourt containers with blackberries and
the dog eating them right off the stem.

We heard the sound of the kids' voices
on Terry Fox Run on the road below.

My past is impenetrable to me
now filled like a thicket so dense

Arthur Bull

that I will never enter it again.
and just when I decide to surrender

and let the past go, some detail
always cuts a path into my heart

like when we all looked up to watch
a jet draw a white line across the sky

This year I didn't plant any herbs
in the two half-barrels by my backdoor

Last year I had basil, chives, sage cilantro,
dill, mint, oregano, parsley, rosemary,

thyme, and tarragon to pick for the kitchen.
I miss them and feel a slight pang of guilt

every time I walk past my back porch.
This year the barrels are full of weeds

and wildflowers: switchgrass, vetch, plantain
dandelion, lamb's quarters, curly dock

Arthur Bull

pretty much like what grows up the hillside
field. Some days I take this as an emblem

of my own decline and some days
I celebrate letting that wildness come

pouring into the barrels from all around
just letting go and letting what happens

happen. but I do miss the crisp flavours
of the herbs on my tongue and still

remember them as a distant pleasure.
And I accept decay along with the old

cracked half barrels which after all
also won't be here very much longer either.

A cherry's deep red
holds a single seed
cradling the future

The enchanted body
of undiluted suffering
draped over her knees

Held and comforted
amid the trembling
of green leaves

Touched by breeze
held tenderly until
he begins to breathe

Arthur Bull

That ditch dry as old leather
leans into the drought, leaving
no trace of bitterness or
regret or remembering
the torrents from rainstorm
that happened a month before,
but sits there, like an ancient teacher
instructing with his silence

Faded red
lanterns torn
paper sway
gently now
to almost
a yellow

matching
September's
hosta leaves.

Arthur Bull

A grassfire begins fast
as a step dancer's kick

takes the dry hillside
with a single match.

That year it scorched
the giant spruce behind

the barn but failed
to kill it. This morning

I watched a crow settle
indecisively on its peak.

I grow old amidst rivers and fog
and stones. Sure, worries don't stop
but here they can take their rest
like the mangy dog on a hot day
sleeping on highway's cool asphalt
that slowly rises and saunters over
to the shoulder just before oncoming
cars then slowly saunters back.
I remember once wanting to be old
at the age of twenty wanting to be
weathered and wise drinking beer
in a Gastown sawdust tavern
one grey morning half a century
ago I can see, the four of us
faded figurines in my memory
arranged along the windowsill
gathering dust like characters

Arthur Bull

in an unfinished forgotten novel.
Now that I'm old I no longer care
about the world and what it thinks
and would not be twenty again
even if I could stand all that pain
How I got through is a mystery and
what I learned a useless question.
The past doesn't matter any more
than the future matters to me now.

How often have I cursed this dark little house?
that holds my grief in its tight grip and keeps
its accurate account of mistakes and sorrows.
How it holds me on a daily track of habits
and lets me never forget my own worthlessness.
Yet I step out onto my porch and look up
at the swaying maples and tall spruces
back behind the barn I take a deep breath
of thankfulness for this dark little house
that's the only place I really want to be.

Arthur Bull

About the author

Arthur Bull lives in Lake Midway on Digby Neck, in Nova Scotia. He has published nine books of poetry and five chapbooks, and his poems and translations from classical Chinese have appeared in numerous Canadian, US and international journals. He is also a musician and has been part of the improvised music scene in Canada for more than 40 years.

As a long-time activist, he has worked primarily with small-scale fisheries and rural development organizations at the local, national and international level.